WITHDR
UTSA LIBRARIES

Lake Songs and Other Fears

Winner of the United States Award
of the International Poetry Forum

1973

Lake Songs and Other Fears

Judith Minty

University of Pittsburgh Press

For Ed

LIBRARY
University of Texas
At San Antonio

Library of Congress Cataloging in Publication Data

Minty, Judith, birth date
  Lake songs and other fears.

  (Pitt poetry series)
  Poems
  I. Title.
  PS3563.I48L3   811'.5'4   73-10035
  ISBN 0–8229–3277–6
  ISBN 0–8229–5242–4 (pbk.)

Acknowledgment is made to the following publications in which some of these poems first appeared: *Atlantic Monthly, Green River Review, New York Quarterly, Poetry Northwest,* and *Story, the Yearbook of Discovery.*

COPYRIGHT © 1974, JUDITH MINTY
All rights reserved
Media Directions Inc., London
Manufactured in the United States of America

Contents

Contents

Lake Songs

Leland

Robert says it reminds him of Scotland
the way waves spume over the seawall
into the still harbor and the bluff
looms black and ominous above. He rode
a gray horse once over the rolling hills
of the peninsula. "Like moors," he said.
"Like home. I was a child again."

On the beach I found a dead seagull,
feathers like fur, so white
they seemed brushstrokes on canvas.
All afternoon I sat with the gull,
let waves rock us back and forth,
watched his outstretched neck, his beak
biting into the sand, his last hold on earth.

The Fourth of July Drowning

They came for you, fumbling through fog,
the half-men, hunchbacked in black suits.
They searched for the echo of your cry,
for your shadow, for your hair floating up
like blind spider legs reaching for light.
Sunless they groped, fins pushing deeper.

Now under siren, through fog
and waves, they bring you to port
hunched, knees drawn up to your chin,
the black bag warm like new beginnings.
Tall women wait cold in the crowd
and remember their arms full of babies.

Independence Day: Leland

It has happened again, another
Fourth of July: waves
crawl hungry at the breakwall;
hunchbacked men in black

hoods drift out over the lake,
as they did that other time,
into gray shrouds. Sirens echo,
the groping begins.

Tonight I will sit on the lawn,
hooded in my blanket, and watch
the celebration as rockets
sink into explosions of stars.

It will be a memorial
to you, your sinking
into that other blackness,
a final explosion of our lungs.

The Island: For Ronald Riker

The snakegrass curled on my desk
begins to yellow at the joints.
Withered, it looks more alive
than when I stole it from South Manitou—
that thieving island that swallows
inward in circles to deserted lighthouse,
to the Rikers who live there alone
without a son, to the cry of obsessed gulls.
In this curling heat I put together
the segments, quickly before fear starts.

Lake Michigan

This lake is cruel.
I drowned here when I was ten,
slid into this water that runs
up the little finger,
felt arms cradle me, no longer
cried for mother, was sucked into black sleep.

This lake chews at dunes,
bites off chunks of sand,
then ebbs back
as firs lean and topple, their roots
dragging deeper roots
until cellars, kitchens, toilets collapse.

Gulls scream at it
from their rookery, then scatter
to tap-dance on ice floes
in January thaws. In June
they fold their wings back
for long suicide dives.

This lake has a memory. It knows
the fingerprints of my cry.
I strip off my clothes,
fall into the waves. I will
go deep, let it lick my skin,
feel its pulse as we sink again together.

Other Fears

Ludington State Park, Revisited

I remember it like yesterday or the day before, as if twenty-five years had not leapfrogged in between to feed upon my innocence.

Wait, I say to my twelve-year-old daughter. She is the same age as I when I last saw the campground, new breasts budding from limp, cotton T-shirts.

Wait—Wait, I promise—until you see the wishing well —the eagle's nest—and above all, the natural, supernatural amphitheater.

Your grandfather (my own father) then with blond Nordic vitality instead of gray tired-out; then even with rough voice, but face not yet chicken-footed into minute States of the Union;

he'd take me by the hand and tell me stories (or did I only imagine them?) of how the Greeks and other possible ancients had their own similar Broadway.

Ferned tiers reach up the balcony ridge, bidding welcome to a jeering, cheering audience. Mossy stage quivers, waiting to accept the tragedy.

Wait—I will show it all to you. You will sit in the deepest forest holding your breath tightly, until the deer pay you their visitation.

You will climb the railroad-tie steps (higher, higher)— more than 200 of them—until you are over the riverbed and under the eagle eye of the eagle.

You will hop jump leap jiggle and joggle over the stepping-stones around Lost Lake (always found) and I will show you where to beware of the slick, thick quicksand.

And on the Old Logging Trail, I will even litanize to you—as my father (your own grandfather) did before me—the dragging of those ponderous logs to the campground.

Which will you take—the green, black, red, brown, blue —violet? Remember, daughter, that it's white returning.

Be careful on the 200 steps! They're washing away now, wearing out. And the stepping-stones have toppled over. Only the quicksand remains.

The eagle has long since expired to his extinction and so has his nest. But we can stand high on the dunes, daughter, and watch the derricks digging.

The wishing well still stands. Let us hurry, for the water is cool and you can run it on your wrists. But who is Betty loves Joe 1968 and what are these obscenities?

And what is this new species cluttering the trail?—smoking, shouting, dropping their droppings on top of the animal spoor. You need not hold your breath, child, even loosely.

The lumberjacks in flannel jackets are dead, and I'm glad, for the winter whirring of snowmobiles has swallowed their studious, steady saw strokes.

And the natural, supernatural amphitheater now is trampled to its greatest tragedy. Let us go home, daughter. We shall ask your grandfather (my father) to make us another memory.

Flight of the Eagle

I

In my tenth summer, I waited trembling
in a clearing of northern pines
to see the eagle fly.
Gold burned on his feathers
as he watched my vigil, eyes
piercing the shadow of tree limbs.
At last he lifted his wings, spread them wide;
I felt talons let loose of the branch.

He rose, beating the wind,
and swallowed the warmth of the sun.

II

My father came for me through heat waves,
wearing a band of mourning.
The blond down on the back of his hand
lifted in the wind
as his fingers wrapped round me.
We walked over burning sand,
high to the top of the dunes,
to stand ready under a barren pine.

From his nest, the eagle
answered my cry.

III

The eagle has flown before
deep into the eye of the sun
to roost at the right hand of gods,
bolt of lightning tight in his claws.
He has ridden on shields and armor,
screeching the cry of war.
His head has replaced the Evangelist;
his wings have supported the word.

He has captured the souls of children
who pour nectar from golden cups.

IV

Guardian of the mountain,
he has sealed the one from many.
But the eagle has fed long on the land;
his eyes no longer see visions.
Now rainbows burst in his throat,
the branch trembles, fear
is like falling arrows.
There are no more vigils, no more fathers.

The souls of a hundred children
are sold in the market as feathers.

The Legend

for D.M.

I

The arrow pierces buffalo hide.
Clouds rise as the tribe moves south.

Warriors' faces glow streaks of lightning.
Thunderbirds soar to the moon's eye.

The canoe glides over still water.
Ravens touch the ripples with greedy wings.

II

It is not forgotten.
     see it flame in the campfire
     see rabbit carry the scent
     see it heavy in the womb of the squaw
     see the infant suckle it from her breast
     see deer run with the message
     see it wait in the wood of the totem
It is there.
     hear it groan at the hunting ground
     hear cayote howl it to the wind
     hear it whisper through pines
     hear it roar out of rivers
     hear snake rattle the words
     hear it weep in the prairie grass
It is everywhere.

III

In Peshabatown

> Amos Kingbird mourns bones in
> the graveyard of his Chippewa
> brothers
>
> Raymond Shocko counts railroad
> ties as he stumbles home with
> his whiskey bottle.

Bear Walk

The Bear Walk, sometimes called "going in fire," is a mystic ritual used by Indians of the Great Lakes region. Its purpose is to cast an evil spell on enemies.

Tonight I will
dance for you,
you whose smile
jewels cow-dung.
I will wear my bear
skin in your honor.
You who speaks
with forked tongue
will be amazed
at the performance,
for my step
will be slow,
my gestures noble.
The chant will hang
on moonthreads.
You will know.
When lights flash
from black fur
and the wind roars
and the earth rocks,
then you will cross
yourself, trembling,
and know surely
that your heart cracks.
Beware the bear
who walks night's path.
She spews out evil
in her wrath.

Eye of the Stone

from the Ojibwa

All things live.

The willow lives.
She brings forth green leaves
and bends to the windsong.
The water lives.
He leaps over fins of fish,
he crawls over land.
The quartz-stone lives.
I polish the stone,
he lives. The eye of the stone
gleams in my hand.
The copperhead lives. His eye follows me.
He glides over stone and sand into water.
He hides in long branches of the willow.

All things die.

The tree turns brittle.
It weeps brown leaves.
The water is still.
Ice halts the water's dance.
The stone falls from my hand,
it dies. The eye of the stone
is buried in dry leaves.
The snake sheds its skin,
curls in upon itself.
The memory of head touching tail,
the memory of polished stone,
of water and green leaves
live in the eye of man.

The Sundial Lies in Shadow

The owl hoots.
Snow shudders
on pine branches.
All that remains of summer
are fan fossils
etched
on this Petoskey Stone.

Love, I wither
like fallen leaves
as you stand waiting for flowers
to burst open
in the meadow.

The Turtle

Head out
    head in
and out again
he inspects
    introspects
his world.

Leathery legs
ponderous
weathered
    grip
    his log
disintegrating wood.
Bulging eye belligerently
examines the ant
and the fly
    who buzzes
    lazy circles
one inch away.

    Snap.
    Head in
head out
    and in again
the pattern repeats:
his eye
    watches.

Homage to Mister Bones

385 dreams
        spun round
in that dog-
tired head,
all searching for the door
        the exit
        whirling
to escape.
Minnesota's dawn
hung cold
        almost
like Breughel's landscape.
From the bridge
for a moment
        Henry fancied
he saw three hunters
in the snow and
raised his hand
        knowing.

        Whirl
and rejoice
from the harbor's
dark floor.
        We
do you glory. See!
Three birds watch;
        the fourth flies.

Night Sail

The sail
rattles and opens
cups
fills with wind
balancing
white
a comet
whose tail froths
starless
we come about
heel over
the rail sinks
into silence
I lean
holding a line
daring myself
to be healed
the sail
like a hand
closes
over the moon
we kneel
are baptized
in blackness.

Contradictions

When the sun
blazed white
you gave me
black roses

at midnight
cocks crowed
waves rolled
over the desert

when I gave
you my hand
the stigmata
appeared

blood flowing
in rainbows
over wings
of snowbirds

as you move
from shadow
to shadow
as I

stand on
street corners
begging
for your flowers.

America

It's a hot day today
in Oklahoma.
Sweat seeps through my shirt
in this dried-up dust bowl.
He sits on the porch
as he has for thirty years,
growing arid like the land.
The cane chair grates
and his shoes shuffle
empty circles on the floor.

"Those sandstorms came
from nowhere. Sweet Jesus,
who would've thought
they'd last for twenty years.
Great, swirling black clouds
blocked out the sun.
You couldn't find your thumb
before your face and oh, Lord,
you crunched the grit of sand
when all you hoped for
was to swallow your own spit.
Your eyes, they burned and stung,
and needles bit your skin like chiggers.
The kids howled and the wife cried
and all a man could do
was shovel out, replant,
and shovel out again."

The sun stretches and hits
the roof of the General Store.
Porch boards creak
and the old man wipes sweat
from the creases of his face.
I think I'll buy a beer
in the saloon across the road.
It's a hot day today in Oklahoma.

A Psalm of David

Lord/shepherd
> I sit here in this damned church
> with the fan whirring and the sweat creeping
> down between my breasts. It must be ninety degrees today.

still waters
> Mr. Kramer across the aisle grates his feet
> on the slate; a restless fly
> buzzes the cherries on the straw hat in front of me.

valley/shadow
> My neighbor fidgets, pulls down her skirt so her panty girdle
> growing orange and yellow flowers (Saks $10.95)
> doesn't bloom anymore.

preparest/table
> My God, I could do with a cigarette, one long drag
> then watch the smoke point fingers
> at the stained-glass window (in memory of).

house of the Lord
> This marble knot in my throat is a prison. It locks up
> someone crying. Tonight
> the bed will be cold without you.

forever.

Fire Prophecy

I

Captured by half-men
whose knuckles drag in dirt,
who cower in caves
to watch jagged arrows flash and ignite.

Two sticks rasp in friction
and the carcass
drips grease on blades of grass.

II

Erupted from Vesuvius,
words wither
as it creeps over the city,
turning to charcoaled bones
ancients who huddle in cellars
and mourn their dogs' ashes.

III

Eagle eggs scream, hatch, home in
to muffle the harbor
in feathers of smoke.

Hushed under winter's hood, Dunkerque
burns slowly.

IV

Repent. The seal is broken.
The seventh scroll unfurls, seven tribes
wail as angels trumpet.

Darkness, as it was in the beginning,
lies on Earth's face.
The lake of fire glows, dims,
haloes a rainbow of sinners.

What Will You Be When You Grow Up?

Step on a crack, break your mother's back (Cradled in her arms).
Flight from tunnel to nest, fledgling
lies in the down of blankets,
is feathered by warm breasts.
Ballerina, fluttering as the swan:
hair coiled round steel muscles, the wing split
in slow sinking to applause.

One, two, buckle my shoe (Smothered by her kisses).
Blond snake-curls strike their fangs
at baby brother who stands in the doorway
and shrieks from pinches on his arm.
Brilliant violinist on a darkened stage:
taloned fingers peck at strings that wail
as her bow saws the instrument in half.

Eenie, meenie, miney, moe (Washed by her tears).
Nuns lift black arms in the specter of death:
Who then will take this woman in holy matrimony?
Worms ooze from her head to creep over stained sheets,
then crawl again into the body
that waits to break her mother's back.

When

When the stone
burns to skip
over cool water,
when murmurs
flail against mouths
sealed mute in mock penance,
when fingers
tremble to touch
your face eyes lips,
your hand,

remember.
The moment
glides through narrow light.
Yesterday
dies in the shadow
of butterfly wings.

Ann Arbor Car Ferry

Twenty-eight crossings a week
Michigan to Wisconsin.
She carries their cars like cattle
back and forth, bow to stern.

Rivers of straw hats and cameras
flow out of her jaws into heat
that bubbles the pores of her skin,
sears even the rails that hold her.

Old girl of the lake, aching
of sailors washed howling to seas
with arms stretched out
to no one, to stars:

now she passes the Frankfort lighthouse,
red beacon striking at starboard,
and lists to port, to port.

Canada Goose

The goose has been living
on our lake for a week. When feet
snap dry leaves, she scuttles,
blankets herself in reeds.

We peer out from shore,
try to tempt her with grain, but she
blends gray feathers, black head
in sheets of shadow and water.

Each Michigan fall I wait for them
to come honking, for those great V's
that point south. I want to see
them homing, farther than I can go.

Indians say the wild goose lives
thirty years, mates for life.
Now she starts her long wait
alone in the first snowfall.

November Morning

It is all too familiar:
Bare oaks huddle together
like aged men whispering on corners.
Ragged giant clouds
carry bundles on their backs.
Our boots sink, crunch
empty holes in the white path.

How many Novembers have we walked this way,
never seeing until now
blood creep outward on the snow
like a Rorschach beetle,
never hearing until now
children who cry inside charred trees,
never feeling until now
the weight of clouds on our breath.

I'm so tired.
Let me wait here
to run blind in the first blizzard,
to freeze quickly
in the craters we have made.

Love Song, Leo to Pisces

The fish swims round the lion's cage;
encircling, circling, tighter, tauter.
Eyes, never shut, guard my ponderous efforts.
Will you save me when the shot is fired?

African grasslands distantly beckon,
the cave darkens, cubs mew.
I have only bars to count, pace off.
Hear me roar to run after the wind.

My heat, too hot, sears the scales
of your skin. Keep a distance.
The ambers, topaz burn,
turn in upon themselves to feed my greed.

Your blues, sea greens
float round the circle, ever constant.
The moon is in the seventh house,
Neptune's fork ascends, the signs

converge, my sun begins to doubt itself.
What have I given you—a little warmth,
a faltering flame. Has it been enough
to keep you in the long, black water?

My Aunt

She waits in gray circles,
sipping coffee round the chip in her cup.
Evening stores its shadow
in stagnant pools, makes hollow corners

where her elbows wait for ghosts.
She recalls unborn babies,
spreads long arms to past lovers, listens
as years circle darkness.

Soon she must turn on the lamp,
bend her shadow to let in the moth:
the one that batters its wings at her window,
the one that calls her its daughter
and begs for light in the dark night.

The Babies

Sometimes in the night I hear them, the unborn babies,
mewing like blind kittens: those boys
conceived behind steering wheels in dark, farmers' fields;
those girls pumped into life on borrowed beds.

Sometimes I see him, that doctor, scraping away
in the hotel room; the roasting pan carried as if it held
the Baptist's head; the toilet swallowing in anonymous gulps.

Oh, Shirlie, Ann: Do you mourn them, as I do,
now when you cuddle your last aging babies to your breasts?

Enter the World of Pleasure

Neon lights swallow moth wings.
Calliope music floats round,
round blind horses who run with chipped hoofs
against reins pulled stiff to escape.

Screams stretch down from cages. Sinews of hair
snap at eyes that grope for greater thrills
than Crack-the-Whip, Tilt-a-Whirl.
Dodge-em, the deformities displayed in jars.

Silver jingles from apron pockets. "C'mon, little lady,
try it FREE. A PRIZE every time. Pitch til you WIN.
NO CROSS THROWING." Christ suffered nails
for the Queen of Sheba who ripples her ass at the barker.

Shoot out a star. Roll your coin inside any lucky circle.
Alligator Woman thanks her lucky star that the moon
can't burn her skin. Boy With Two Faces
hides his eyes in The Laughing House of Mirrors.

At Bert and Zelda's Midway Cafe
the counterman leers at young girls
and dreams dreams of his own
secret, mysterious rides in his trailer.

Summer Heat

Two weeks since rain. The sun's eye bulges.
Dust creeps over buildings, bakes on sidewalks.
A mongrel bisects the avenue and wearies himself
toward the puckered shade of wilting elms.

From his tight row of houses, Leroy Johnson
waits behind windows that waver hot.
He sweats for wind fingers that will
tumble over pavement and lift lace curtains.

He yearns for tomorrow when perhaps the baby
will not cry and his wife will come
to stand in the doorway, white slip silhouetted
against brown skin. Together then, perhaps tomorrow,
they can sit on the porch and count raindrops.

Going Home

A streamer on slender arms, the highway
salutes horses who graze through blurred fences.
If the children were with me,
I would point to the mare's delicate legs,
her flicking tail. I would tell
how once I rode bareback, the coarse hair
of the mane tangled in my fingers.
This road measures more than miles.

Billboards leap out, speckling cornfields:
The Wagon Wheel. White Lake Marina.
Waves, alone on the October beach, roll up,
greet me. Through a flash of dunes and grass
I see hands touching, bare feet running
on the sand, his fingers entwined in my hair.
Soon I must pass the cottages, then oak-lined streets,
to the door that opens past blurred fences.

My Father's Watch

Every evening, he wound the watch
that was his father's
and looked deep into its face.
Nordic hands, puckered from scrubbing
my brother's back and mine,
carefully turned the stem.

Bath-clean in my nightgown,
I stood waiting for his sigh,
for the click-shut of the case.
"Where's my girl?"
I'd run into his arms,
into his beard's rough stubble.

I returned, a woman, to find him
hunched in his chair,
gold watch open in his hand.
My throat turned rough.
"Papa, what do you see inside that case?"
There was fire in his hand
as he opened his arms again.

Driving Through Fog

As I drive through tunnels of fog here in Michigan,
car lights no brighter than tails of fireflies, I remember
the other drive, all night, how I groped along the Sunshine Parkway.

Then I was homing. I think I could have done it blind,
that stroking through dense, jasmine-scented seas. It was a return
for me, back to the tunnel I had swum from
in the beginning, to her Catholic faith,
a rocking again, a glimpse of day after long nights.

But when in that darkness did I know
I was suddenly older than she—that sun and moon
glint only in patches, that there is no beam to light such tunnels.

Ashes, Ashes

I

Near Norway's Stave Church, protected
by the Vikings, lepers
shuffle snow puffs along their special path.
They watch the mass through window holes
and, fingerless, cross themselves.

II

Old soldiers march neatly in regiments
in Paupers' Cemetery. Lifted
from the stain of county beds, caissoned
to winter plots, now their hands stay
crossed under white blankets.

III

Forever children, Maria Sanchez
and Annie Fergus lie quiet under the brittle tree,
touch fingertips with maple roots.
Their wooden crosses tilt as thinly
they sing Ring Around the Rosy.

IV

In this cold climate, it is difficult
to grow daffodils on holy land.

Making Poems

for Rita

I have a friend
who lives in an old shoe
of a house with many children.

When she grows hungry for poems
she opens her recipe box,
her pantry of images,

sifts out bat wings,
snake tongues, monks' beads,
the root of a tree.

She mixes, stirs, incants.
She measures the words
in cups and tablespoons.

I think she has the power
to cast spells. Those poems
fill my head like warm bread rising.

The Cats in the Barn

"Diese Katzen be killers!"
The chicken dead
and the cats still there
in the fray of feathers and clucking.
And Herr Muller bellowing,
the gunnysack already in his hand.
Those hands,
weathered from milking cows
and counting hens' eggs
in countless half-dawns,
the knuckle creases lined
with soil from his potato field.
His fury making even his blond
mustache tremble; those hands
grabbing at the cats by the neck
legs tail, stuffing
them into the bag; those
hands that lay gentle on my shoulder
when I came for visits to his barn.
I saw what he was going to do.
The cats mewing, him roaring,
a twelve-year-old girl wanting to run,
but pressed instead against the barn wall.
Those hands banging
the gunnysack against the post,
the cats howling, screeching
in their darkness. The sun
stabbing my eyes, me whispering
to him to stop,
begging the cats to stop crying,
wishing those hands to be still.

The Horse in the Meadow

I saw him, that wild stallion,
when I dressed in white. He galloped
along our ridge at dusk,
ran against the sky's flame,
mane and tail streaming
fine strands before dark clouds.

Here, he grazes in the meadow
where birds sing yellow songs,
where the wind blows in circles.
Coat damp, glistening, his flanks
burn as he paws at grass
and listens for thunder.

She is dressed in black, that old crone.
She leans on the fence, cooing,
reaches out with bony hand
and offers him sweets.
I know her. She wants to
touch those velvet ears, run hands

over that strong back, braid her fingers
in that mane. She wants to
climb on him, break him,
ride him back to her house. She
wants to hobble him, rein him.
She wants to hide him in her bed at night.

If I let her, there will be
no more colors from birds' mouths,
no more lightning in clouds.
There will be no more little girls
who wait in sheets of fire.

Menses

Tied by the umbilical cord
I run, kited into night, rise
and fall in strange pulls and thrusts.
Born under the sun sign,
I orbit a lunatic world

and gather myself in moonwort
to sweeten that period,
that rush of sudden flooding.
These eyeless ovaries, this empty uterus,
have never seen the fullness

of his smile, the fade to a crescent,
the sliver that begins new life.
But, moonstruck, they know.
The belly swells, the nipples
falsely ready themselves. Too late.

Moonseeds spread, stain
the whirring flight of luna moths.
From dark to dark, each twenty-eight nights,
I revolve and harvest myself
through neap and spring tide.

The Legacy

No need to dial the doctor. I have
already heard that it flows in the genes,
floats on invisible electric currents
perhaps, from mother to son
to daughter, the mother again.

I have been to that old barn, looked
up through the dusting sunlight
from loft to splintered rafter; have almost
seen the rope, the empty space full with her
sagging skirt and dangling legs.

I have listened, but they never speak
her name, that grandmother
shrouded in dust, the grave
marked with whispers that sin begets sinner.
I have ceased to pray to the Virgin.

No matter. Yesterday I saw fire
in a cat's eye, touched the coarse mane
of a wild horse, at last set my house
in its strange order. At night
clouds form in front of the pale moon.

Waiting for the Transformation

My daughter is a mystic about cats.
I am afraid. I have seen her conversing with them,
watched her nod, blink her eyes; and the cats
twitch their whiskers, almost smile.
When she was five, she told me that if our old Tom
curled close to the fire, there would be
snow the next day. Often there was.

I think, although I fear to know for certain,
that she becomes a cat at night.
Just yesterday, I saw tiger shadows
on the wall of her room. I hear strange cries
in the house before dawn, feel the rattle of purrs,
a softness that feathers my face.

I do not think about it, tell no one.
I have decided to wait until other children's eyes
glint fire, until they all leave their mothers' arms
and turn wild—howling in the night.

Spell Involving the Laying On of Hands

You must first know by heart the secret
verse. Pass your hands three times slowly
over the hurting place, recite
the words, lay your hands on the wound.
If a person believes, he will be healed.

This hurt is deep. It has something to do with
you. Touch me. Pass your eyes
over my face, place your lips on my
left breast. Find the wound, lay your hands
on it. Listen, the secret verse mentions love.

Upon Seeing the Aurora Borealis for the First Time on My 35th Birthday

For me, the birthday girl, it was a portent.
I waited, almost hoping we would never see those lights.
For the others, it was an excursion
like a carnival trip to see freaks expose their anomalies.
I would have liked red wine, a toast,
a Eucharist even. Instead there was
cigarettes and Scotch, the flash of matches and laughter.

Stretched out on cool sand, the sky spilling stars,
we were first-nighters waiting for the curtain.
I thought of my Nordic father, how he had seen that show
birthdays ago up near the Arctic Circle;
the reverence in his voice as he told
how, like an umbrella it had opened perfectly over his head,
the rays fingering down so close he could have touched them.

And then, from over the lake, it began for us.
First a flicker of candles, then a blaze
of white yellow orange. It was
a blossoming: the petals unfurled, stretched
out from the north in their celebration of beams and arcs;
withering, then brilliance;
silence, then an explosion of light.

It was quiet before terror, before they
began to roll as if alive. I wanted to
shut my eyes, cry out that the umbrella was gone.
Only ghosts now, raining, tumbling, roaring
over each other; years chasing, haunting across the sky.
He said, "I thought the world was coming to an end."
And, papa, it did then—in a way.

Winter Tree

for M.H., 1889–1971

I

It is three years since they uprooted you
from your wilting, flowered chair
and that cluttered house
with its fading wallpaper blossoms;
tore your hands from the basement workbench
where you stood planted
on braided rugs thin with years of feet;
since they sold your furniture and dishes,
drove away your car, gave you back
two pipes to smoke and one blue suit for Sundays.

II

For three years you tried to spread out roots
in that gnarled orchard, the Old Folks' Home;
strained to hear the mumbling man next door
and to read each night's microscopic news;
watched the nuns float over you like birds, white feathers
fluttering, voices cooing, faces downed in prayer;
retreated from your neighbors' twisted fingers
and faded eyes; avoided mouths that ate themselves
and minds that only listened to the past;
saw snow turn to rain and back again;
felt leaves wither, branches tremble.

III

Today we stood in the shade of the chapel
and thanked the fumbling priest who forgot your name.
Then we packed your life
in two brown cardboard boxes: pajamas and underwear
leafed with tobacco, a half-eaten box of chocolates,
the gold watch still keeping time.

Oh, grandpa, old man. The tallest tree
is where the eagle builds his nest.

Why Do You Keep Those Cats?

All winter, those cats of mine
doze like old women in front of the fire,
curl their fur around saucers of sunlight
they have trapped on my rug. Sometimes
they bury themselves in the wool of blankets
to sniff dreams I left there.

Awake, their eyes reflect deeper sleeps.
Delicate tongues yawn, hide needles of teeth.
I listen for their soft paws,
for their purrs to rattle in slow circles
near my bed. They want to capture
warmth from my body. "Why do you

keep those cats?" my neighbors ask.
Why? It is for summer that I wait
for their claws to unsheath, for their eyes
to blaze orange in dark hallways.
Soon they will tear at my door, howl
to walk with lions along the fence.

It is not for winter. It is instead
for the flame of yellow moons.
Then I run wild with them,
hide in trees, sleep again in leaves;
in August I will sink my teeth,
as they do, into the warm necks of mice.

Cat Lady

There are too many dead rabbits
outside my door, severed legs and heads.
The cats bring them. Howling,
they circle the house,

make paths with their claws, rub their fur
against my door. They want me
to take their gifts, let them in.
Their eyes glint like daggers in the dark.

I am afraid. I will no longer
put on my coat, walk out among leaves.
My windows bear steamy messages
to neighbors who will not answer.

There is nothing else to do. I draw
a circle of bones on my kitchen floor,
step inside and rock myself.
No one can get in anymore.

Blue Baby

Sister of the congenital heart, meant to be
two years younger than I,
playmate for swings and dolls.
You, Patricia, doll of my parents'
love nights, there was no time—blue death
staining lips and fingertips, creeping
toward the murmur in your nursery crib.

Without you I grew, whispered to your shadow,
played sister to our dolls—
and saw you often, deep
in the garden of our mother's eyes.
Still I bloomed, forgot you
until my guilt matured: a blue vine
that twists now in the pulse of my heart.

Where Is the Poet in This Poem?

I know this poem. For years
it has been waiting in dark hallways
like a prostitute looking for tricks.
Notice how it chokes and coughs up mothers
who wring their hand and moan to the Agnus Dei.
Remark that there is no father present.

This poem licks all erotic zones simultaneously.
It has mated with unicorns, but always
discharges an imperfect fetus.
Nuns carry a cross through the streets of its veins.
Blind men tap their canes against corners
in the hexagon house of its skull.
Like the moment of death, it remembers every person
it has known, every word ever spoken to it; yet
all images wither as they touch air.

The earth is separating somewhere.
I stretch taut under the skin
of this poem, fly about inside its body.
I knock at its teeth eyes ears, crying to be let out.
This poem is no Miss America Doll. It's me.
God damn it, this poem is me.

Making Music

Tuesday afternoons in the cave of our basement
my mother, like an organist,
sat in front of the old white mangle,
her music heaped in a wicker basket beside her.
I saw the flash of fur under her arm

as she lifted a sheet, folded it twice, and with her knee
moved the pedal that made her instrument go.
I watched wrinkles feed into the mangle, heard a hiss
as heat met dampness of muslin, smelled soap under scorch,
saw clean hymns flow out of the roller.

I have no talent for music, am not my mother.
Two hours by car from Kalamazoo to Muskegon
I sit behind the wheel, direct my instrument
along a white line, around curves, over rises;
my pedal maintains a tempo of seventy miles an hour.

Headlights rest on the fur of dead animals, and my wheels
roll over them: rabbits, cats, squirrels
pressed into the sheet of highway. It is a long drive home.
The hum of my motor blends with the thump of bodies
and the static rock beat out of the radio.

PITT POETRY SERIES

COLOPHON

These poems have been set in Granjon types by Heritage Printers, Inc., of Charlotte, North Carolina, and printed directly from the type on Warren's Olde Style antique wove stock. The book was bound in Kivar 5 by John H. Dekker and Sons, Inc., Grand Rapids, Michigan. It was designed by Gary Gore.

5426 127